PROMONTORY'S LOCOMOTIVES

Gerald M. Best

Introduction by
HORACE M. ALBRIGHT
FORMER DIRECTOR — NATIONAL PARK SERVICE

Golden West Books

P.O. BOX 8136 • SAN MARINO, CALIFORNIA • 91108

PROMONTORY'S LOCOMOTIVES

Copyright © 1980 by Gerald M. Best
All Rights Reserved
Published by Golden West Books
San Marino, California 91108 U.S.A.
Library of Congress Catalog Card No. 80-15895
I.S.B.N. 0-87095-082-7

Library of Congress Cataloging in Publication Data

Best, Gerald M.
Promontory's locomotives.

1. Locomotives — United States — History.
2. Railroads — United States — History. I. Title.
TJ603.2.B47   625.2'61   80-15895
ISBN 0-87095-082-7

COVER PAINTING

The cover painting is a somewhat different view of the completion of the first transcontinental railroad with the driving of the Golden Spike. The artist was asked to depict the startling vastness and solitude of the wasteland where this significant chapter of American history occurred. The time, 2:30 P.M. — the date, May 10, 1869. The artist of this painting is Howard Fogg of Boulder, Colorado, nationally famed illustrator of railroad subjects. This art was prepared for the May picture of Union Pacific's 1969 color calendar commemorating the Golden Spike Centennial year. — COURTESY OF THE UNION PACIFIC

BOOK ILLUSTRATION

All the photographs appearing in this volume were taken by the author as a record of the building of the new *Jupiter* and *No. 119*. The historical photographs dating back to the Golden Spike ceremony are from the author's collection or that of the publisher. Data for the profile of the Pacific Railroad in the Promontory area comes through the courtesy of the Southern Pacific Company and was made from their official historic profile.

Golden West Books

P.O. BOX 8136 • SAN MARINO, CALIFORNIA • 91108

INTRODUCTION

When the West's Central Pacific met the East's Union Pacific at Promontory on May 10, 1869, our first transcontinental railroad was completed. With the driving of the "Golden Spike" America's railroads literally became the life line of a growing nation.

For 32 years hard-working steam locomotives climbed the grades on each side of Promontory Summit. Finished goods and those wishing a new life in the American West rolled westward, while raw materials moved east. In time the single-track main line to the scene of the "Golden Spike" lost its status as a new water level line across Great Salt Lake was opened in 1903 known as the Lucin Cutoff. From this time until 1942 the Southern Pacific, successor to the Central Pacific, maintained the old line as a branch, finally its rails were torn up.

Historians and souvenir hunters scoured the old right-of-way for nearly a century. Finally the Southern Pacific erected a stone monument to the "Last Spike" at Promontory during the 1910 era because of the interest. The site was again glamorized in 1944 with the issuance of a 3-cent postage stamp honoring the 75th anniversary of the "Golden Spike" ceremony. Railroad buffs and tourists alike trampled through the range land and dry farms in search of the monument and a glimpse of the old grades. Local residents even held a mock spike driving at the site each year on the 10th of May.

Through the efforts of various Utah organizations, headed by residents of Box Elder County, in which Promontory lies, the Utah Historical Society, the Utah Pioneer Trails and Landmarks Association, and others petitioned for some permanent facility with the 100th anniversary only a few short years ahead. At long last, Congress passed legislation declaring the Promontory site as a "National Historic Site" under the supervision of the National Park Service.

All organizations in Utah banded together in search of history and artifacts, the Southern Pacific donated the land for buildings, parking lots, access roads, and the right-of-way for a number of miles to each side of the site. Between 1965 and 1969 the National Park Service built a beautiful visitors center and several hundred feet of track at the spike-driving site. Old steam locomotives were borrowed from museums to re-enact the driving of the "Golden Spike" daily during summer months. The 100th anniversary celebration was a huge success with more than 25,000 citizens in attendance. Interest in Promontory grows each year by leaps and bounds.

Today, the Golden Spike National Historic Site has its own replica operating steam locomotives and this most interesting volume tells the story of their design, construction, and operation at Promontory.

As a former director of the National Park Service, I have seen many historic places, just like Promontory, set aside for all the public to enjoy. I hope the significance that the "Golden Spike" driving at Promontory, 111 years ago, had on our nation and the growth of the American West will live on for all time. I am reminded of the words engraved on the original spike which said, "May God continue the unity of our country as this railroad unites the two great oceans of the world."

Horace M. Albright
Former Director
March 17, 1980   National Park Service

PROMONTORY'S LOCOMOTIVES

by Gerald M. Best

Few events in American history have captured the nation's imagination as did the building of the first transcontinental railroad and the celebration of its completion with the driving of a golden spike into a laurel tie at Promontory, Utah, May 10, 1869. Two beautiful steam locomotives, the *Jupiter* of the Central Pacific Railway and *No. 119* of the Union Pacific Railroad nosed toward each other and touched pilots in the desolate landscape. Not a man there doubted that this moment was among the nation's finest. The continent was bridged and the United States was now truly one nation.

The two chief engineers of the railroads, Montague of the Central Pacific and General Dodge of the Union Pacific, shake hands as the *Jupiter* and *No. 119* touch pilots on that historic day, May 10, 1869.

This monument was erected at Promontory by the Southern Pacific, successor to the Central Pacific, in 1919. It was moved from its original location, as shown here, to its present site in 1968.

Once the golden spike happening was completed, little mention was made of the celebration except for a few lines in the history books. The two famous steam locomotives were not saved and worked out their useful years, as will be mentioned later. The Southern Pacific (successor to the Central Pacific) erected a monument at Promontory to historically note the event in 1919. Although later the old Central Pacific line via Promontory was abandoned and the rails removed, the monument remained in the middle of a field. While off the beaten track, thousands of historians and railroad enthusiasts drove to the site yearly. With interest increasing year by year, Mrs. Bernice Gibbs Anderson of Brigham City organized, some 30 years ago, a group of local residents to re-enact the driving of the golden spike at the historic location each year on the 10th of May.

With the 100th anniversary of the golden spike driving less than four years away, Congress designated Promontory as the Golden Spike National Historic Site on July 30, 1965. Plans were laid out for a visitor center to be completed by May 10 of 1969. Replica locomotives of the *Jupiter* and *No. 119* were part of an overall plan to develop Promontory to its near original appearance. It is the purpose of this book to explain how two brand new 4-4-0 type steam locomotives, exact replicas of the *Jupiter* and *No. 119* came to be built, the story of their construction, and the search for substitute locomotives until the new engines could be delivered to Promontory.

After May 10, 1869, and until the sale of the Union Pacific track from Promontory to Ogden, all trains of both railroads terminated their runs at Promontory. A station, restaurant and other facilities were built just east of the golden spike site and were maintained until a short-cut route, under the name of the Ogden-Lucin Cutoff, was built across the Great Salt Lake in 1903. This saved the Southern Pacific 44 miles in distance and provided a water level track. Service on the old Promontory line was reduced to a branch line mixed local daily, and the tracks were finally removed in 1942.

The people of Utah began making plans to celebrate the Centennial of the Golden Spike in 1965. The Department of the Interior was also warming up to the potential of a permanent facility at Promontory and the national importance of the 100th anniversary. A square tract of land at Promontory and the old Central Pacific right-of-way were donated by the Southern Pacific Company to create the historic site. The National Park Service then obtained an appropriation from Congress to build a museum center, and hoped to include two replica steam locomotives which could face each other in front of the museum. The spike driving ceremony would then be held several times during the day. Immediate plans included an elaborate ceremony to be held on May 10, 1969, with future plans containing the relaying of track and an operating railroad.

During March of 1966, Roy Appleman, then Chief of the Branch of Historic Studies of the National Park Service, came to California and called on the author. He was searching for information on the two original locomotives that met at Promontory, the *Jupiter* and the *No. 119*. His investigation included such material as locomotive erecting plans or data, photographs, or any type material that would aid someone in building two steam locomotives. A deadline was set for the completion of two replicas and delivery was to be within three years, or in time for the Centennial of the Golden Spike. Since steam locomotives were no longer manufactured in the United States as a commercial product, this was a tall order. Erecting drawings would have to be made quickly and a contract let to a responsible locomotive builder.

The author was able to supply a number of photographs of Central Pacific's *Jupiter* class engines, and in due time was able to certify the exact date the *Jupiter* was placed in service. On hand were photographs taken at the Golden

Spike Ceremony held on May 10, 1869. Four photographers were there that day. They included A. A. Hart of Sacramento who came to Promontory on the Central Pacific special; Andrew J. Russell and his assistant S. J. Sedgwick photographing for the Union Pacific; and Colonel Charles A. Savage, a Salt Lake City commercial photographer who specialized in local scenes. The Russell photographs, all made on large 11 x 14-inch wet-plate glass negatives have been published in countless books in recent years, and a few Sedgwick photographs appeared under the Russell name. It was not until the late Lucius Beebe and Donald Duke, the publisher of this book, each on separate explorations of the attic of the American Geographical Society in New York, discovered the vast Sedgwick lantern slide collection and a few original negatives. This rich find included many unpublished photographs of the Union Pacific during its construction. Many of these historic scenes appeared in my book on

Photographs of the Golden Spike ceremony as taken by S. J. Sedgwick from the roof of the *Jupiter's* cab, on May 10, 1869.

the locomotives of the Central Pacific and the Union Pacific entitled *Iron Horses to Promontory,* published in 1969 as a monument to the 100th anniversary of the Golden Spike. A. A. Hart used a stereoscopic camera with two small negatives side by side, producing the well-known three-dimensional pictures when viewed through a stereoscope. Hart's stereo prints were small and do not enlarge well when copied, but provide a wealth of locomotive details.

Several weeks passed before a locomotive draftsman of considerable talent was engaged by the National Park Service to provide detailed locomotive erecting drawings on a crash basis. The deadline and the lack of any engineering drawings proved too much for the draftsman, who after making 50 of the 500 drawings required for pattern making, had a nervous breakdown. He was so broken up he burned all the tracings and prints, though he did return the research material. Thus the two replicas of the Promontory engines died on the drafting table as there was not time left to build two operating steam locomotives for the 1969 celebration.

The Centennial of the Golden Spike, to be held at Promontory on May 10, 1969, would have been anticlimactic without steam locomotives on hand for the reenactment of the spike driving. With replicas out of the question, a search was begun by the National Park Service to find two 4-4-0 type locomotives that looked like the *Jupiter* and *No. 119*. Once again the author was called upon to help in the search for two locomotives.

The Pacific Coast Chapter of the Railway & Locomotive Historical Society owned the former Virginia & Truckee Railway No. 12, the *Genoa,* which closely resembled the *Jupiter.* This 4-4-0 type built by the Baldwin Locomotive Works in 1873 was loaned to the National Park Service by the Society. It was sent to the Southern Pacific's shops in Sacramento and modified as much as possible to look like the *Jupiter.* It made a presentable substitute and was a near twin except for the lack of a solid brass steam dome cover. To represent the Union Pacific No. 119 another previous Virginia and Truckee 4-4-0 type, the *Reno* No. 11, owned by Metro-Goldwyn-Mayer Studios was loaned for the Centennial. After a thorough face-lifting operation by the Union Pacific at their East Los Angeles Shops, it closely resembled Union Pacific's No. 119. While these two Baldwin-built engines differed in some respects from the original Rogers and Schenectady designs, they both served their purpose and performed well for the Centennial of the Golden Spike.

The two substitute locomotives remained at the Golden Spike Site until MGM Studios requested the return of *No. 119* in July 1969. When the summer season was over, the stand-in for the *Jupiter* was returned to Sacramento where it is now on exhibit in the California State Railroad Museum. Without two real locomotives on display at Promontory, the National Park Service felt interest in the Site would be greatly reduced the following year. To remedy this situation, two other former Virginia & Truckee Railway locomotives, Nos. 18 and 22, were borrowed from Paramount Pictures in Los Angeles. The Union Pacific had previously borrowed these

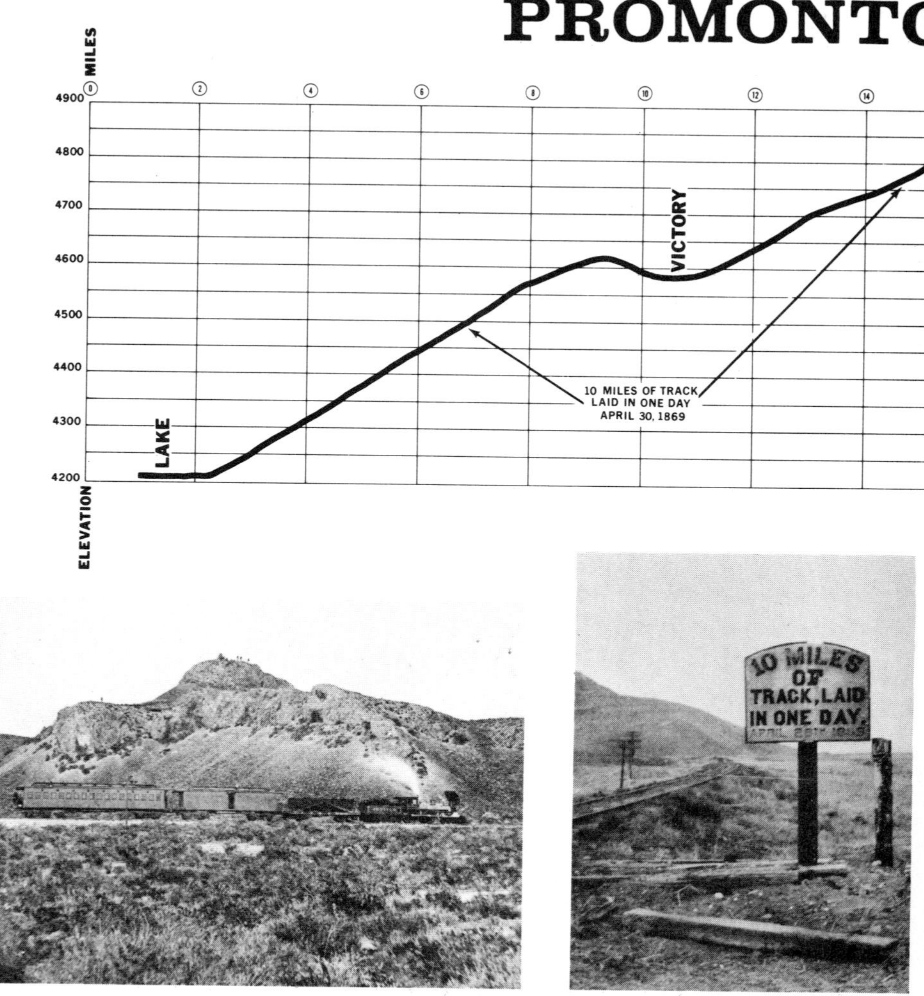

Promontory, the site of the driving of the Golden Spike, is located at the summit of the Promontory Mountains. Locally it is called Promontory Hollow. The profile shown above indicates the average percent of grade eastward from Lake to Promontory was 1.17, while westward from Blue Creek to Promontory it was 1.30. (ABOVE LEFT) The *Jupiter* at Lake, the start of the climb to Promontory. (ABOVE) The sign erected in 1869 at the east end of "Ten Miles of Track, Laid in One Day." (ABOVE RIGHT) Promontory Station as it looked during its brief life as a terminal of the two railroads. (RIGHT) The great Union Pacific trestle erected in haste in 1869 a few miles east of Promontory. Its approach fills are visible today.

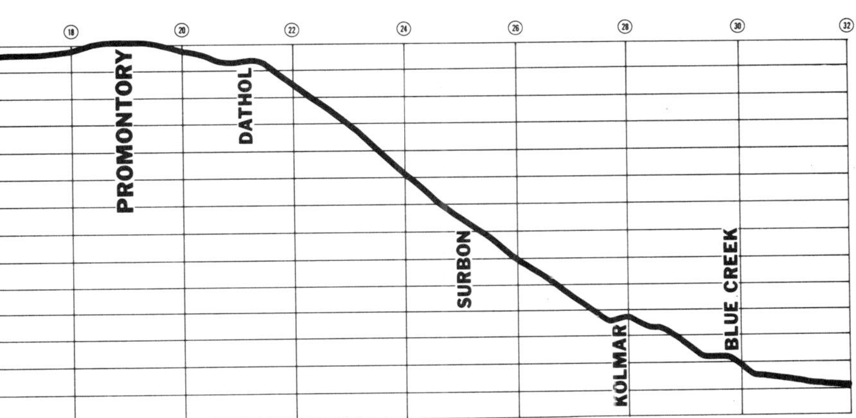
18
20
22
24
26
28
30
32
PROMONTORY
DATHOL
SURBON
KOLMAR
BLUE CREEK

R.R.
CAR 7
650

Union Pacific's Centennial display train with replicas of the *No. 119* and *Jupiter* at East Los Angeles in 1969. These engines were on exhibit at Promontory from 1970 to 1978.

engines during the spring of 1969 for promotional purposes. They were painted to resemble the Promontory engines, then loaded aboard flat cars facing one another, and sent all over the Union Pacific System as an exhibit train as part of their Centennial publicity program. This provided the Golden Spike Site with two locomotives for the summer of 1970.

Although the Paramount engines were eventually sold to the State of Nevada a few years later, the two substitute engines remained at Promontory delighting the visitors until the end of the 1978 season. At this time, they were trucked to Carson City, Nevada, to be placed on exhibit at a future date. Long before these engines left Promontory the National Park Service long range plans for the Site had been set in motion. The Golden Spike National Historic Site had to have its own steam locomotives, preferably exact replicas and operable.

Through great effort on behalf of the citizens of the State of Utah and their many friends in Washington circles, an appropriation for the making of erecting drawings and of forming casting patterns for two operating replica steam locomotives was passed by Congress in the early 1970's. Bids were solicited and the contract awarded to the O'Connor Engineering Laboratories of Costa Mesa, California. While this firm's main products are accessories for the motion picture and television industry, its president, Chadwell O'Connor has wide experience in the design and construction

12

of large steam operated power generating plants. Not only did he have a Master's degree in Mechanical Engineering, but he was also a steam locomotive buff. O'Connor had his own steam locomotive and assisted in the rebuilding of other engines for his friends with backyard railroads. He and his assistant, John Healy were completely capable of building steam locomotives from the rails up. O'Connor believed he could produce sufficient detailed drawings to erect two full size locomotives and have the casting patterns made within a year's time.

Steam locomotives are no longer used on North American railroads, except in tourist train service. While the steam boiler is still popular in industry and there are more steam boilers in service today than ever before, it is difficult to find people familiar with both steam boilers and the mechanics of the steam locomotive. Under the terms of the contract between the National Park Service and O'Connor Engineering, your author was selected as an Engineering Consultant and National Park Service Representative for the making of the drawings and patterns.

Chadwell O'Connor, the president of O'Connor Engineering, signs the contract for the locomotive drawings in March 1975.

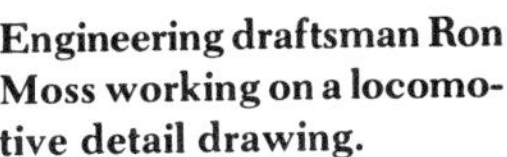

Engineering draftsman Ron Moss working on a locomotive detail drawing.

Work was begun on the first stage of the erecting drawings by April 1, 1975 and the first set of drawings were the complete outline of both locomotives and tenders. From these basic drawings the detailed drawings would be made from data obtained and the use of photographs. Unfortunately the Southern Pacific, which had absorbed the Central Pacific, had sold the original *Jupiter* in 1893. Naturally, the locomotive drawings were no longer available. The Union Pacific had thrown out their drawings of the *No. 119,* no doubt at the time the last of its class of five engines was scrapped.

Research located an outline drawing of one of *Jupiter's* mates, made in 1895 before it was rebuilt, and thus saved the day by offering many of the basic dimensions, the number of flues, and the overall engine and tender length. Files in the Union Pacific museum at Omaha provided the principal dimensions of the *No. 119* and these were invaluable in preparing the basic outline of the engine and developing the working drawings. In fact, the two locomotives were quite similar in many respects while coming from two different builders.

The National Model Railroad Association prepared to honor the Centennial of the Golden Spike long before the event. They offered prizes to members who built the best scale models of the *Jupiter* and *No. 119.* There being no drawings for use by the competing model builders, the organization had to prepare suitable drawings of the two engines and as a result the author was involved once again in helping William R. Plunkett of Pasadena, who had been asked to make the drawings. With the aid of the basic engine dimensions and the use of photographs, Plunkett prepared beautiful drawings of both engines. After appearing in the Association's *Bulletin,* they were fully reproduced in the author's book *Iron Horses to Promontory.*

Photographs proved to be an invaluable aid in working up the detailed drawings of locomotive parts. Views of a number of Schenectady engines built to the same drawings as the *Jupiter* were located. The builder erected ten engines for the Union Pacific and three for the Rensselaer & Saratoga Railroad in 1868. These differed from the *Jupiter* only in the use of a diamond stack for screening coal cinders instead of the bonnet type used on wood burning locomotives.

Fortunately, the photos of the three Renesselaer & Saratoga engines were full left side views, whereas the Russell photographs were all right hand side views. Using the known dimensions of the drivers and certain other features, a scale could be established and all the other parts measured and included in the basic drawings.

Photographs of Union Pacific *No. 119* and its four mates (Nos. 116-120) did not provide a full side view, but several three-quarter angle photos of Nos. 116 and 120 were found. Details for the *No. 119's* Bissell type lead truck and many other parts were obtained from the drawings of a Rogers 1867 4-4-0 type locomotive in a book by Zerah Colburn published in London in 1871. The well-known book of locomotive drawings by G. Weissenborn, published in 1870, was used extensively even though the book did not include any Schenectady drawings. All material used by William Plunkett in the preparation of the National Model Railroad Association drawings were turned over to the O'Connor Engineering Laboratories. Soon the basic dimension outlines of both engines were made and approved.

Railroad buffs came to the aid of O'Connor once they learned of the project. The valve gear for both engines was designed and drawings of each part were made by Morrie Houser, a design engineer for WED Enterprises (a Walt Disney Company), during weekends. Houser had designed the valve gear for many of the Disneyland steam locomotives, and it is a tribute to his skill that when assembled, the valve gear for both replicas fitted into place perfectly.

Many of the wooden patterns for the locomotive parts were made in the shop of Wayne Helmick, a personal friend of O'Connor and another enthusiast. He made the patterns for the driving wheels, tender and lead truck wheels, the cylinder block and the many small patterns for the valve gear. The same pattern was used for the cylinder blocks of both engines by means of an ingenious design whereby the cylinder sections of the pattern were on a pivot, held in place by metal pins. After the cylinder block for the *Jupiter* was poured and cast at Commercial Iron Works in Los Angeles, with the cylinders in a horizontal position, the pins were removed, the cylinders slanted about two and one-half degrees toward the rear of the block and the pins inserted into other holes to keep the cylinder section rigid. A second

Some of the finished wood patterns for the valve gear. These are used for the making of a mold into which molten metal is poured to form a casting. Both locomotives required many patterns for the various parts of the engine.

Wood patterns of the driving wheels. From the pattern on the left four driving wheels were cast for the *Jupiter*.

casting was then made for the *No. 119*. The use of this method saved considerable money. After the principal patterns were made, Helmick sold his business and went to work for O'Connor to finish other patterns and construct the two locomotive cabs. They were made out of the finest seasoned birch, a true cabinet-maker's job. To show off Helmick's beautiful craftsmanship, the cab of the Union Pacific *No. 119* was stained instead of painted.

George Westinghouse did not patent his locomotive air brake until 1869, hence the *Jupiter* and *No. 119* were not equipped with this revolutionary railroad appliance when the two locomotives met at Promontory. As built, both engines had hand brakes located on the rear tender truck only and operated by the fireman. In the days before air brakes, the fireman and engineer of a light engine would work as a team, the fireman applying the hand brakes on the tender and the engineer reversing the engine. With the cylinder cocks open and the throttle cracked slightly, the engine could be brought to a halt at a specific spot. The thought of braking engines today by this means was looked upon with disfavor by the National Park Service just for safety's sake.

The idea of two live steam locomotives was to re-enact the Promontory ceremony once a year, just like it was done on May 10, 1869. Bringing two engines together today without air brakes brought visions of smashed wooden pilots. O'Connor had to recreate the drawings of the air compressor used by the Pennsylvania Railroad on the trial run of the first automatic air brake. He had to work from available information, have patterns built and castings made. Once this was accomplished the castings were machined and pumps assembled. The air compressors for the two locomotives were mounted on the side opposite the viewing audience during the pageant. To do this the *Jupiter* had its compressor mounted on the left side, while the pump for *No. 119* appears on the right side. The storage tanks for the air are concealed as much as possible at the rear of the locomotive fireboxes. The two brake valves for the engine air and the train brake line are placed low so they are not visible from the ground.

The construction or erecting drawings of the two locomotives were completed on schedule during April 1976. Sets of blueprints were provided the National Park Service and to any firm wishing to bid on the building of two steam locomotives. Major American locomotive builders had not turned out a steam locomotive since 1955 and all their huge machinery was geared to building diesel-electric locomotives. The only firms interested in the construction of the replicas were amusement park railroad builders. Because of O'Connor's vast knowledge of steam locomotives and working experience with steam boilers, the O'Connor Engineering Laboratories was awarded, in October 1976, the contract to build two steam locomotives to be delivered in late 1978, using the drawings already prepared.

A large section of the O'Connor factory building was refitted for the erection of two locomotives, standing side by side, on adjacent tracks. Steel rails were set in the concrete floor with the track extending outside so that the tenders could be assembled independently from the engines. While O'Connor had a well equipped shop, it did not have the facilities for the machining of large engine frames, cylinder blocks and other heavy work necessary to complete a locomotive. Fortunately, being located in Southern California, which is a highly industrialized region, all these services were available within a 50-mile radius.

When the *Jupiter* and *No. 119* were originally constructed, the engine frames were made from sections of wrought iron or steel bars, bolted together. For the replicas, the frames were cut out of one single plate of steel at the U.S. Steel Company's plant in Huntington Park, California, giving the new engines added strength. The L&F Industries machine shop, just a few blocks distant, successfully completed the long and tedious job of machining the frames to exact size. L&F Industries also machined the cylinder blocks, bored out the cylinders to a 16-inch diameter, machined the pistons, cylinderheads, crosshead guides and many other parts of the two locomotives.

In the period of time since the *Jupiter* and *No. 119* were built, locomotive boilers have changed greatly. In olden days boilers, after being formed into cylindrical shape, were riveted. Today, the seams are electrically welded to increase the boiler's life and safety. The boilers for the replicas were built at the Dixon Boiler Works in Los Angeles. Dixon had built many special boilers for steam locomotives, including the boilers used on the engines of the Disneyland railroads. Dixon's job was made easier as both boiler shells were of the same diameter, had the same number of two-inch flues and except for the extended smokebox on *No. 119,* the boilers looked alike at a distance. All seams in both boilers were welded to comply with the rigid State of California Code, even though the engines were to be operated on government property in another state. Rivet heads were welded at the

At the left, *Jupiter's* boiler at the Dixon Boiler Works in Los Angeles. The flues have been installed and the welder is working on a brace fitting. (RIGHT) Grinding the rough edges from the staybolt heads on the boiler of *No. 119.*

Bob Dowty and Bill Fowler test a pair of the *Jupiter's* drivers for alignment.

Union Pacific *No. 119* in the assembly stage at O'Connor Engineering Laboratories of Costa Mesa, California. In this scene, the cylinders have been bolted to the frames, and the lead truck is in place. The driving wheel pairs have been fitted into their axle boxes and the counterbalance weights installed.

seams of those parts of the boiler which are visible to the public, such as the smokebox. Each boiler is licensed for 160 pounds of steam pressure, as compared with 135 pounds steam pressure on the original engines. Since the new engines have no cars to haul, the lower pressure will probably be used to save fuel. These custom-made Dixon boilers took more time to complete than a standard industrial boiler, thus delaying the completion date of the engines by six months.

Steam locomotive driving wheels consist of the centers, which are machined to size, and the tires, which are of steel and are first heated, then shrunk on the wheel centers. When the wheels are mounted on the axles, the drivers on the right side must be quartered, or rotated 90 degrees with respect to the drivers on the left side. Until steam locomotives were replaced by diesels, machinery for quartering each pair of drivers was available in every large shop. Today, the Southern Railway shops in Birmingham, Alabama, has the last known machine able to do this operation. The Southern agreed to machine the eight driving wheels, order steel tires and to fit them on the wheel centers, mount the wheels on the axles and quarter the wheels on the right side. In the interest of safety, O'Connor decided that the driving wheels should be made of steel, even though the originals were made of iron.

The steel driving wheel centers and the wheel castings for the tender and lead trucks were completed by the West-electric Steel Company of East Los Angeles. They were then shipped to the Southern Railway in Birmingham. A few months later all the wheels were returned, mounted on axles, drivers equipped with steel tires, ready for installation. The small castings for the valve gear, crosshead pumps, head-light brackets, etc., and the tender frames were made at National Steel & Shipbuilding Company in San Diego.

With the arrival of the parts, O'Connor's crew set out to assemble the *Jupiter* and *No. 119* reproductions. With the frames set up on blocks on the floor, the cylinder blocks were fitted, axle boxes installed and everything readied for the driving wheels. Eight driving rods had been made at L&F Industries, and during that time, O'Connor had completed the bronze bushings for the axles, the yokes were installed, and as soon as all the valve gear parts arrived, the machinery

Union Pacific *No. 119* outside O'Connor Engineering for a progress photograph. The driving rods and crossheads are completed, and the boiler is ready for lagging (heat insulation). (LEFT) *Jupiter's* boiler backhead with many of its fittings in place.

of the two engines began to take shape. After the boilers were mounted on the frames, they were lagged and metal jackets applied. The latter were painted to resemble oldtime Russian iron as close as possible.

Many of the finishing touches for the two engines were made by Fleming Metal Fabricators of City of Industry,

Union Pacific *No. 119* had its wooden pilot built on the locomotive instead of separately. In this view, the exhaust manifold may be seen in the center of the smoke box and the curved steam pipes have been fitted.

While under construction, the *Jupiter* was rolled outside for a steam test. A temporary stack was made of welded oil barrels since the engine's bonnet type stack would not clear the doorway of the erecting room. The new boiler jacket, the polished brass handrails and jacket bands are in place. (BELOW) General view of the erecting shop of O'Connor Engineering, with the cabs in place on both engines. The erecting crane was portable and used for handling the heavy locomotive parts.

The Central Pacific *Jupiter* in the final stage of completion. Its cowcatcher has been installed and waits for the painter. Note that the cab has been removed for detailing. The tender has been rolled into the shop for lettering.

25

The *Jupiter's* bonnet stack is ready for its coat of black paint.

California. These included the smokestacks, tender tanks and other sundry parts. The stack for the *Jupiter* is huge, as can be seen in the many photographs, and this bonnet stack is a work of art. The cabs for both locomotives were made of wood. Wayne Helmick, a master carpenter, began the project, but had to retire before the cabs were completed. Buck Marron, another fine cabinet maker finished the job. They looked so nice unpainted that it was a shame to cover up the craftsmens' art. Sheet copper was applied to the cab roofs, just like their prototypes. Marron also built the wooden pilots, window frames, cab seat boxes, tool boxes and the headlight platforms.

The headlight of Union Pacific *No. 119* has been painted and gold leaf decorations completed. Only the reflector and lamp are missing.

The cabs for the two engines were built on the floor of the locomotive shop, and are shown here with their first coat of varnish. The cab for Union Pacific *No. 119* is at the left. (BELOW) The cab for *No. 119* is now in place with the panels painted a bright red. Later, unpainted sections were stained darker, but were left unpainted to show the natural wood.

The rear tender truck for the *Jupiter,* before the brake rigging was installed. The leaf springs at the top were standard for most locomotive builders at the time. The *Jupiter* was built by the Schenectady Locomotive Works.

The frame and trucks of Union Pacific *No. 119's* tender, ready for the water and fuel tanks.

The completed tender of *No. 119,* ready for painting and lettering. The tender was designed to carry coal, although the Union Pacific burned anything they could get their hands on as the rails neared Promontory in 1869.

The tender trucks and their frames were assembled outdoors behind the shop building, while the bulk of the small machine work was done by O'Connor's facility under the direction of Keith Frey. The locomotive assembly and fitting of parts was supervised by foreman Bill Fowler. Many of the fittings and simulated forgings were made by Mike Monroe, an expert in the art of welding. The complete project was under the direction of Chad O'Connor and his assistant, John Healy.

As the two reproductions were nearing completion during early April of 1979, volunteer labor on weekends was gratefully accepted. Many rail enthusiasts and historians

The finished boiler of Union Pacific *No. 119,* with an authentic Rogers bell frame, hand painted sandbox with oil painting and gold leaf, and polished steam dome cover. The vertical cylinder on the left hides the boiler check valve, a decoration soon abandoned by locomotive builders.

Ward Kimball, a railroad buff and an original Disney Studio animator, finishes one of the oil paintings on the rear of Union Pacific *No. 119's* tender.

wanted to have some little part in the completion of these famous locomotives. The gold leaf ornamentation and lettering of both engines, the striping and the creating of four paintings on the sandbox and tender of Union Pacific *No. 119* was done by a crew headed by Ward Kimball of Mickey Mouse fame. Ward was one of the original animators of the Disney Studio and a railroad buff all his life. He was assisted by Rudy Lord of WED Enterprises (WED standing for Walter E. Disney) and Rich Saychala of Disneyland who is an expert on laying gold leaf. Kimball was presented with a problem at the last minute with regard to the oil paintings on both sides of the sandbox of *No. 119*. In one of the original Russell photographs, the sandbox is quite visible, but when this section is blown up to large size to see the subject matter of the painting, it turned fuzzy. A group of Disney artists looked at the enlargement and there were mixed opinions as to the subject of the painting. One group thought the man was Johnny Appleseed picking fruit from

31

The cab of Union Pacific's *No. 119* is a sight to behold. Note the hand painted decorations with raised letters and numerals.

an apple tree. Another group said it was a man with a rifle standing near a tree, such as a hunter. Unfortunately, no picture of the right hand side of *No. 119's* sandbox exists. Hence we did not know if the same painting appeared on both sides of the sandbox. Kimball solved the problem beautifully; he painted the hunter on the left side, with the fruit picker on the right side. The paintings at the rear corners of *No. 119's* tender tank were difficult to duplicate. With the aid of photographs, he used a painting style contemporary with industrial machinery paintings of the 1860's and the end results are admirable.

All Rogers locomotives had the maker's name on a polished brass plate above the cylinder. This picture shows the slanted cylinder and crosshead guide; a design which Rogers retained until 1870.

The *Jupiter's* air pump is installed on the left side of the engine. It is patterned after the first Westinghouse air brake compressor.

In 1868 the Schenectady Locomotive Works was still using wood brake shoes for the tender brakes, whereas, Rogers used iron. In this picture are Jupiter's four brake shoes, handmade and ready for installation.

The *Jupiter* and *No. 119* are perfect examples of American locomotive builders' art. It was only from about 1845 to 1870 that this elaborate style of painting was in fashion. Highly finished locomotives fell from favor shortly after the driving of the Golden Spike primarily because of cost. Another factor was the introduction of coal burning and its sooty smoke which soon covered the engine's brightwork with grime. (ABOVE) The Central Pacific *Jupiter* has just been delivered to Promontory, and is ready for the dedication ceremony. The engine number 60 is carried on the sand dome and number plate on the front of the smokebox. (RIGHT) Union Pacific *No. 119* stands resplendent in the brilliant morning sun at Promontory. The date is May 10, 1979, dedication day, and the 110th anniversary of the driving of the Golden Spike.

The locomotive headlights were hand made at a sheet metal works, painted and gold leafed by Kimball's crew. The bells and their frames, the whistles, the front number plates and all the other detailing such as handrail posts were custom made. The only commercial products on the engines are the steam gauges, throttle valves and the boiler water glasses. Kimball redesigned the faces of the steam gauges with etched antique numbers and letters of the 1868 period.

Originally the *Jupiter* burned wood for fuel and the *No. 119* burned Wyoming coal. While the purist will criticize the use of fuel oil, it was more practical for each engine to burn the same fuel and have it readily available at the Promontory enginehouse. Both locomotives use a new type of burner built by the Laidlaw-Drew Company of Edinburgh, Scotland. They build the only type burner for locomotive boilers that is not visible outside the ash pan. They have proved to be extremely quiet, smokeless and economical. Even with petroleum at high prices, cordwood is becoming more expensive than oil, and like coal, difficult to handle, requiring ash pits in the enginehouse with frequent cleaning of smokebox screens and boiler front ends.

The tenders of the *Jupiter* and *No. 119* were brightly painted like the locomotives. In the scene above, the *Jupiter,* lighted by the morning sun, is on display for the admiring crowd on dedication day. The engine is half way in the enginehouse. The *Jupiter's* tender had less ornamentation in the rear; a gold leafed rectangle with a vermillion striped rectangle inside. Four years after it was built the tender was painted black. (BELOW) Tender view of *No. 119* showing the gold leaf striping and ornamentation.

The right side of the *Jupiter* at Promontory on dedication day. The bright paint and polished brass glisten in the late afternoon light.

The highly polished, solid brass steam dome cover of the *Jupiter* is in sharp contrast to the painted sandbox with its gold leaf ornamentation.

Following the dedication ceremony, the *Jupiter* and *No. 119* are admired by the invited guests. The engines were not used in the annual ceremony because the connecting tracks had not yet been installed. (LEFT) The front view of Union Pacific *No. 119*, a replica of which the builder should be proud.

As the time drew near for completion of the replicas, an enginehouse was erected at Promontory so the locomotives could be serviced and protected from the weather. This structure stands approximately 3,000 feet east of the Golden Spike Site and contains all the equipment necessary to do routine maintenance. Two small, watertube boilers were built by O'Connor to be placed in the enginehouse. One of these boilers is kept hot all the time to provide quick starting each morning, and to provide heat for the building, as it is often below freezing at Promontory in the winter. When the locomotives are not in use, they are stored with the boilers full of treated water to prevent rust and deterioration. This same chemical will be used in the boilers at all times during operation of the engines to prevent boiler scale.

The men who built these engines are proud of their work, as well they should be. Two of them, Robert Dowty and Bill Fowler have moved to Brigham City and will be in charge of the two engines. If they need repairs, these men will surely know what to do, as they were on the construction job from the beginning. After the enginehouse was completed, a contract was let for the laying of track from the enginehouse, on the roadbed of the old Union Pacific main line, to connect with the already existing track at the Golden Spike Site. A "wye," which is used for turning engines around, was also built at the enginehouse area. This work was completed early in the summer of 1979, and with the arrival of the engines, the fundamental plan for Promontory has been realized.

60
JUPITER
C P R R
JUPITER

CENTRAL PACIFIC No.60 *Jupiter*

PRINCIPAL DIMENSIONS

Builder	Schenectady Locomotive Works	Driving Wheels	62-inch including 2½-inch tires, 57-inch wheel centers
Type	4-4-0 American		
Diameter of Cylinders and		Wheelbase	Rigid — 8 feet
Stroke	16 x 24-inch		Total — 21 feet 6½ inches
Boiler	Shell — 50-inch outside diameter	Weight On Drivers	39,000 pounds
	Firebox — 66¾ x 36 x 66-inch	Total Engine Weight	65,400 pounds
	Flues — 179 of 2-inch diameter	Water Tank Capacity	2,000 gallons, approx.
	and 11 feet long	Fuel	Wood

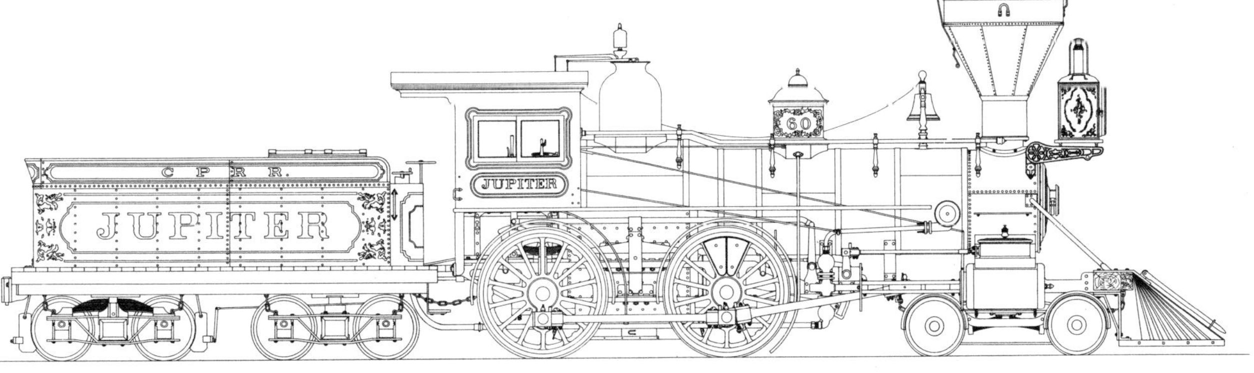

— COURTESY O'CONNOR ENGINEERING LABORATORIES

UNION PACIFIC R.R.
119
Nº 119
ROGERS

UNION PACIFIC No. 119
PRINCIPAL DIMENSIONS

Builder	Rogers Locomotive and Machine Works	Driving Wheels	57-inch including 2½-inch tires, 52-inch centers
Type	4-4-0 American	Wheelbase	Rigid — 7 feet 9 inches
Class	BK-4		Total — 21 feet 9 inches
Diameter of Cylinders and Stroke	16 x 24-inch		Engine & Tender combined 41 feet 10 inches
Boiler	Shell — 50-inch outside diameter	Weight On Driver	41,800 pounds
	Firebox — 66¾ x 36 x 66-inch	Total Engine Weight	68,400 pounds
	Flues — 179, 2-inch diameter and 11 feet long	Water Tank Capacity	1,942 gallons, approx.
		Fuel	Coal

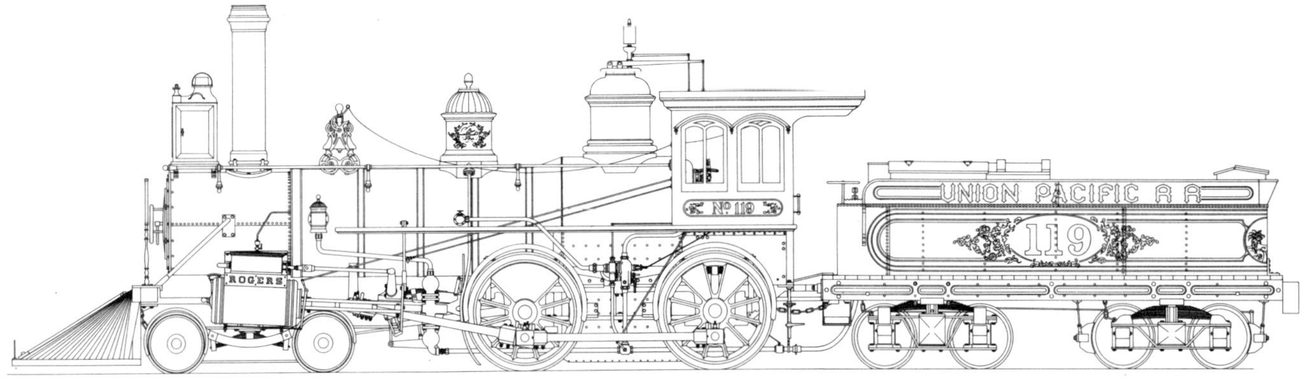

— COURTESY O'CONNOR ENGINEERING LABORATORIES